I0430114

Applied Psychology

Volume 11

EFFICIENCY

FACTORS

Being the Eleventh of a Series of Twelve Volumes on the Applications of Psychology to the Problems of Personal and Business Efficiency

BY

WARREN HILTON, A.B., L.L.B.

FOUNDER OF THE SOCIETY OF APPLIED PSYCHOLOGY

**ISSUED UNDER THE AUSPICES OF
THE LITERARY DIGEST
FOR
NEW YORK AND LONDON
1919**

**Republished from the public domain
by**

Creative English Publishing

www.Creative-English-Institute.com

Under Classic Reads

May 2014

**ISBN-13:
978-1499593365**

**ISBN-10:
1499593368**

CONTENTS

Efficiency Factors

FOUR SUCCESS-FACTORS AND THEIR PRODUCT

Chapter I

FOUR SUCCESS-FACTORS AND THEIR PRODUCT

SUCCESS ELEMENTS PREVIOUSLY CONSIDERED

WHATEVER the phase of practical life in which you are engaged, there are, in addition to the strictly mental requirements for success dwelt upon in previous books, certain more or less outward or material characteristics that are of considerable importance.

The factors we have already considered, grouped under somewhat different heads, are (1) Self-Analysis, (2) Singleness of Aim, (3) Self-Mastery, and (4) Character.

APPRAISING YOUR CAPITAL ASSETS

(1) Self-Analysis. — You must try to appraise your static self — that is, to ascertain by systematic introspection the amount of your present personal capital assets — (a) your experience and your present practical ability and knowledge as distinguished from your innate capability; (b) your command of your own powers. What kind of man are you and what kind of man ought you to be at your time of life, with your experience, with your opportunities and with the abilities you know that you possess?

(2) Singleness of Aim. — You must plan your career definitely and completely.

SINGLENESS OF AIM

Men continually fail for lack of a definite aim. Their desires are as wide as the field of life, and what they attain to is largely a matter of accident. Many a man is the spoiled favorite of a blundering good luck.

The man that from day to day centers himself on one thing at a time, while keeping always in the background of his thoughts the long-run aim, makes an imperious demand on the world's treasury.

In the words of William Wirt, "The man who is perpetually hesitating which of two things he will do first will do neither. The man who resolves, but suffers his resolution to be changed by the first counter-suggestion of a friend — who fluctuates from plan to plan and veers like a weather-cock to every point of the compass with every breath of caprice that blows— can never accomplish anything real or useful. It is only the man who first consults wisely, then resolves firmly, and then executes his purpose with inflexible perseverance, undismayed by those petty difficulties that daunt a weaker spirit, that can advance to eminence in any line."

ACQUIRING GREAT POWER
OVER OTHERS

(3) Self -Mastery. — You must govern yourself, for only in this way can you acquire great power over others.

To be a truly strong man you must be steady and purposeful. You must conserve and utilize your psychic power.

Mind-power makes the man.

Mind-power scientifically unfolded, controlled and directed makes the self-mastered man.

ELEMENTS OF THE DEEPER SELF

The self-mastered man can do anything humanly possible.

Mind- power self -developed, self-controlled, self-mastered, needs but intelligent direction to become invincible.

(4) Character. — We are creatures of habit. Factors (1), (2) and (3) determine conduct, and conduct molds character.

The world demands of him who knocks at the door of opportunity an unimpeachable integrity and a character bedded in granite.

Ambition, pride, self-improvement, I self-reliance, promptness, enthusiasm, reliability, honesty, breadth of view, winning personality, creative imagination — all these must be elements of the deeper self.

COMMERCIAL REGOGNITION OF CHARACTER

Yet it is a self that can be trained.

Our regimes for psychic power and initiative, followed incessantly, persistently, with confidence, will determine habits of thought and action until in time that which these habits constitute — character — will fix them as the only thinkable or permissible courses to pursue.

In time the whole personality will be exalted and fortified against lapses, and will shine forth for its worth to be commercially recognized.

All these factors of Self-Analysis, Singleness of Aim, Self- Mastery and Character that we have been considering are purely mental.

They have to do solely with the mind. But there are certain outward and more or less physiological matters that demand the attention of the success-seeker.

These are (1) Dress, (2) Address, (3) The Language of (Business, and (4) Health.

We now proceed to analyze these factors in detail.

DRESS AND ADDRESS

Chapter II

DRESS AND ADDRESS

OBTAINING AN INTERVIEW

CLOTHES do not make the man. But they make all that is seen of him, except his hands and face, during business hours.

A man's clothes must be clean and must be appropriate to the kind of work in which he is engaged.

First impressions are of immense importance.

If you look prosperous, and the man you are dealing with is attracted by your appearance, you have gained a great advantage.

ESSENTIALS OF OUTWARD ATTRACTIVENESS

The well-groomed, well-appearing man who looks self-respect and prosperity is seldom denied an interview.

It is a fact of common observation and experience that men like to talk to persons who look healthy, active and well-dressed. Dress for comfort is an evolutionary development from dress for adornment.

The instinct for display is primarily sexual, but attractive articles of dress as worn by men have been in all ages and in all stages of civilization the rewards of individual skill and prowess. This is as true of the well-dressed business man today as it was of the savage with the scalp-lock at his belt.

Ornament with men means that the wearer is a formidable person. It is a sign of wealth, success, ability and power, and a potent means of obtaining a high rating with others.

JEWELS IN A RAG-BAG

Dress shabbily, and the world will assume that you are pigeon-livered and lack courage and have never achieved anything.

The world will take you at your own valuation. Who, then, keeps a precious jewel in a rag-bag?

Dress quietly. Wear clothing of fine quality but plain color. Remember Beau Brummel's axiom, "To be well dressed, you must not be noticed."

PSYCHOLOGY OF CORRECT CLOTHES

In very truth, this axiom contains the whole psychology of dress as applied to success in your relations with others, since if you are noticeably shabby or noticeably overdressed the effect is to distract attention from yourself and what you have to say and unfavorably direct it toward your clothes.

With shabby clothing it is difficult to command favorable attention; with loud clothing it is hard to inspire confidence.

The psychic importance of being well and appropriately dressed is two-fold: first, for the impression you create in the minds of others; second, for the reactionary effect upon yourself.

No man can do his most effective work in his dealings with others unless he is dressed as he thinks he ought to be dressed. In your own office, or in another man's office, this mental satisfaction and its reaction upon your own work is worth looking after.

THE MAGNETIC PERSONAL ATMOSPHERE

To attain to perfection in dress you must analyze your needs for correctness. You must cultivate an unobtrusive originality. You must adapt your apparel to the occasion, to the time of day, to the surroundings and to the people with whom you come in contact. You must make an outward sign of your business activity, your enterprise and your good breeding.

Thereby you will avoid unfavorable comment and will obtain the respect of others, an increased self-confidence, a more magnetic personal atmosphere and a greater all-round efficiency.

A good address includes courtesy, tact and self-restraint.

ELEMENTS OF TACT

Tact is a quality which serves its possessor well at all times and under all circumstances. All persons regard it as a thing greatly to be desired, but many fail to recognize that it may be consciously cultivated.

Tact when analyzed is found to be made up of certain elements.

It means the ability to put one's self in the place of another and see the matter with his eyes. It means the ability and willingness to yield for the sake of expediency. It means the forbearance to patiently await the opportune time for vindication. It means the kindheartedness to refrain from voicing such sentiments as would needlessly offend. It means the gracious acceptance of unavoidable situations. It means gentleness, magnanimity, cheerfulness and a sympathetic knowledge of the fears, weaknesses, expectations and inclinations or human nature.

THE MAGNETIC PERSONALITY

Courtesy consists in part of good manners. Good manners are the reflections and the shadows of the inner virtues.

A courteous address will at once place you on the high road to favor and success.

"Give me but one hour," said Wilkes, the politician and journalist, whose ugliness was as remarkable as his charming manners and address, "and I shall not be one inch behind the handsomest man in all England."

A courteous address opens doors that are closed to good looks, wealth and fame. And it will keep them open.

It is the first step that counts. The man who knows how to take it enters everywhere upon a firm footing, while the boorish and hesitating blunderer is lost.

HINGES A BUSINESS CAREER TURNS ON

Courtesy is a positive quality. It is more than a mere lack of discourtesy. It is the outward evidence of an inward sense of justice and a respect for the rights of others.

In all history little things have been the hinges on which careers have turned. A merchant is impressed by the unfailing "Thank you!" of a news- boy and employs him, and the lad becomes a master of finance. A smile of recognition wins a friend, and so admits one to a wide circle of men and women who contribute to his social and material advancement. Acts of courtesy and thoughtfulness are the seeds of opportunity, and any day may find the harvest ready to be reaped.

THE AMENITIES OF BUSINESS

The contrary is equally true. 'A valuable business connection was lost because a man so far forgot himself as to criticize the entertainment afforded by his host. One can never tell what alluring prospects may be erased from the landscape of one's future by a lack of regard for the little courtesies of life.

We sail a dangerous sea. One variation from compass or chart may end in disaster. Only by the most careful seamanship can we hope to reach the haven of success. But if every turn of the helm represents our best effort, any day, any hour, may bring the glad cry of "Land ahead!"

THE LANGUAGE OF BUSINESS

Chapter III

THE LANGUAGE OF BUSINESS

PRIME ELEMENTS IN BUSINESS LANGUAGE

THE world of work moves at high pressure. Consequently the element of greatest importance in business language is economy. Short-cuts, slang, abbreviations for technical phrases, all pass current as good business English and all evidence the demand for swift conveyance of thought.

The purpose of all business language is to convince the intellect and win the heart.

USE OF STOCK PHRASES IN CORRESPONDENCE

Consequently, good business language adapts itself where possible to the social customs and the degree of culture, refinement and intelligence of the person addressed. It talks to him in his own terms, and it is sometimes most effective when it is most replete with slang and symbolism.

When it comes to business correspondence eliminate such useless phrases as "We beg to inform you," "We beg to advise," "In regard to same," etc.

There are hundreds of such stock phrases that not only do not get you anywhere, but actually weaken the force of what you have to say. The ideal letter is the one that most nearly represents the writer, and no man uses this sort of stilted jargon in conversation.

NINETEEN PRACTICAL SUGGESTIONS BASED ON ACTUAL LETTERS

Every such phrase adds to the formality of a letter and detracts from its personal quality.

Charles R. Wiers, chief correspondent of the Larkin Company, is quoted in "Caxton" as giving the following suggestions, the phrases in italics being taken from actual business letters, and that which follows being the revision by Mr. Wiers:

"We would say. We would state. If you have something to say, just say it. Beating around the bush takes all the — ginger out of a real message. Enclosed — herewith. 'Herewith' means the same as 'Enclosed,' hence a repetition of no meaning. We have investigated our books and find, etc. Of course, you have investigated, or else you could not reach an accurate conclusion. It is always best to state a thing definitely instead of weakening it by one or more preliminaries that do not mean anything. We shall be glad to receive your, further patronage. Patronage can hardly be called a commercial term, and at the best it is too big for a business letter. Use the word 'favors' in preference to patronage, as it is simpler and means more. Allow us to explain. Permit us to advise you. Will you pardon us if we venture to call your attention to, etc. If such expressions are proper, then it is somewhat absurd to request permission and state the explanation in the same letter. It would be more in order to write one letter and ask your customer if you dare to explain something to him, following it with the explanation after you have received his permission. The good correspondent goes ahead and does his explaining with the knowledge that the other man is busy, therefore wants his explanations and everything else delivered to him by the shortest route possible.

"We have your favor of the 24th, contents of which have been carefully noted. Probably there is nothing so often repeated to no advantage in business letters as this nonsense about 'contents have been carefully noted.' Nobody can explain the reason for it. All we know is that it has been an heirloom among business letters, and as a result we have continued to use it without any thought as to its meaning. The omission of it will improve the beginning of a letter, and incidentally help one to be watchful over the remainder. We have now balanced your account and will consider the transaction closed. We have balanced your account. The transaction is closed. One or the other of these expressions would cover your point. Not necessary to use both at the same time. We are entering an order for the and it will he shipped, charges prepaid. Your will be shipped, charges prepaid. We wish to explain our terms. Just go ahead and explain them. Never mind the preliminaries. An early answer will be greatly appreciated, as we wish to adjust this matter to your satisfaction, also sending the missing goods without additional expense to you. As we wish to adjust this matter satisfactorily, an early answer will be appreciated. So we may balance your account in full, and close our records of this transaction.

So we may balance your account.

"Our records here in Buffalo show. — Our records show. Arrangements have now been made. No point to any of this. The job of a correspondent is to tell a customer just what has been done in the fewest words possible. Preliminaries foreign to the real point are simply a waste of time and money. We are entering your order and will send you postpaid. We will send postpaid. Upon receipt of this letter we trust you will, etc. 'Upon receipt of this letter' is unnecessary, because the customer couldn't do much, if anything, until he knew what you wanted. At the present time we cannot locate. At present we cannot locate."

TALK THAT WINS MEN OVER

No business man talks to his customers and associates in the way the average business man writes to them. And yet a letter is merely a talk, and should be as fluent, free and to the point as if writer and reader were face to face.

To be a successful business correspondent, one must know men's minds. The object of a letter is to influence conduct, and to do this well you must be able to get the other man's viewpoint and read your letter with his eyes.

When you dictate a letter picture your correspondent as sitting before you while you talk to him. If you do this, you will never say to him, "I beg to advise you."

SEEING THE MAN BEHIND THE LETTER

Form a mental picture of the man you are writing to. Study his letter to you with a view to estimating his education, his opinions, his financial condition. Sometimes a word or phrase, the arrangement of the headings, or the capitalization will help you to see the man behind the letter. Sometimes you have to go to outside sources of information. But you may absolutely depend upon it that unless you do visualize the man you are writing to you cannot write to him with any great effectiveness.

Efficiency Factors

HEALTH AS A FACTOR IN EFFICIENCY

Chapter IV

HEALTH AS A FACTOR IN EFFICIENCY

FUNCTIONAL AND ORGANIC DISEASES

WE ADVOCATE mental control as a means to functional health of the body. In doing so we have no desire to disparage or belittle other hygienic and therapeutic agencies, or even to institute a comparison.

We do not maintain that all diseases can be cured by mental means alone.

The reader is presumably well grounded in the course of reasoning from which we concluded that all bodily functions are under mental control, that this control is capable of being exercised through consciousness — that is, consciously as well as unconsciously — and that the secret of absolute mental control is concentration.

Distinguished authorities on pathology agree that a practical discrimination may be made between functional and organic diseases. This distinction is not strictly scientific, because there can be no perversion of action on the part of a bodily organ without a change of cellular structure, just as there can be no thought in consciousness without an impulse to physical activity.

Yet, for all practical purposes, the distinction is an intelligent and proper one. An organic disease, like consumption, is one involving a real loss or destruction of organic tissue. A functional disease, like neuralgia or constipation, is one in which there is no actual loss of tissue, but in which one or more organs of the body fail to perform their normal functions or perform them in an abnormal manner.

RANGE OF UTILITY OF
MENTAL METHODS

Generally speaking, mental methods are chiefly of use in cases of functional disease. In organic ailments they may relieve pain and may help the forces of repair, but with persons of only average concentrative ability mental exercises cannot be depended on unaided to speedily and certainly cure organic maladies.

We learned long ago that the subconscious control of bodily processes is exercised in accordance with such sensory images as are emphasized by the conscious attention.

Every functional disease, being a perverted form of organic activity, is therefore due primarily to false or misleading intelligence from the central consciousness to the vital organs.

Every thought complex has its emotional element.

Every thought tends to express itself in the appropriate bodily activity with which it is associated.

Every idea is a pent-up reservoir of physiological impulses that will work themselves out in full development unless inhibited by contrary ideas and impulses.

Therefore, a consciousness that is clear, definite, harmonious and concentrated will bring about automatically some kind of prompt, appropriate and complete bodily response.

And the more vivid the picture, the more unclouded by conflicting thoughts and impulses, the more immediate and complete will be its physiological realization. For every thought you hold tends to manifest itself in bodily action.

This will be made clear by illustration. Thus, a disgusting story may take away your appetite for the most delicious repast. It may interfere with the digestion of what you have already eaten. It may even cause nausea. The reason for this is because you hold in consciousness the thought of the story and its loathsome associations, and the digestive organs are unable to discriminate between actual present sense-perceptions and suggested imaginings, between the real and the simulated, and they react accordingly.

So far as bodily organs go, consciousness — whether it be a consciousness made up wholly of ideas or a consciousness of sense-perceptions — is the only reality.

It follows that the digestion, indigestion or rejection of food by a normally constituted stomach is in the final analysis a question of mental attitude. Stated generally, the immediate cause of abnormal or perverted action by any bodily organ is abnormal or perverted mental action.

INFLUENCE OF BLOOD SUPPLY

A second fact of great practical importance is that all processes of secretion and repair in the body are directly dependent upon blood supply.

Blood furnishes to every living cell the food necessary to its life and to the performance of its special function. Consequently, the continued life and health of the body presupposes a plentiful supply of blood. And for the same reason the stimulation of any particular organ to special activity necessitates an increased circulation of blood in the part indicated.

Blood results from the consumption and assimilation of air and food. The quantity and quality of the blood depend upon the quantity and quality of the air we breathe and the food we consume and the extent to which both are utilized by the organs of assimilation and elimination, such as the lungs, stomach, kidneys, liver and skin.

TWO ESSENTIALS FOR GOOD HEALTH

It follows that the first requisite of good health is an abundance of good air and good food.

How these and all other material blessings are to be had through mental control has already been indicated in Volume Ten. In the present volume we must assume their supply.

Granting an abundance of good air and good food, the next requirement is that they shall be consumed and assimilated.

Consumption and assimilation imply respectively appetite and the performance in a natural and efficient manner by each bodily organ of the function for which it was designed.

DEPENDENCE OF VITAL OPERATIONS

Since abnormal or perverted action on the part of a bodily organ is caused operations by abnormal or perverted mental action, it follows as a corollary that the normal performance of the vital functions cannot take place without a normal and sympathetic mental attitude.

To illustrate: If you are unable to digest some article of food that is readily digested by the average healthy person, it is because somewhere in the recesses of your mind, perhaps only in some organic plexus, you hold the thought that you cannot digest it.

You may not think you do so. You may not do so consciously.

You may have merely a feeling of repulsion.

SECRETION OF CHEMICAL RE-AGENTS

Yet somehow, somewhere, as a result of some past experience, you are obsessed with the idea that you are unable to assimilate this particular article of food. And the idea of that food is inseparably bound up in a mental complex of feelings and impulses, not of appetite, enjoyment and digestive processes, but of fear and doubt and inhibitions of the impulses necessary to the secretion of the fluids required for digestion and assimilation.

A lack of appreciation of the mind's influence has led physiologists into unfortunate errors.

Thus, because in experimenting with animals they have been able to cause the gastric juice to appear by tickling the lining of the stomach with a feather through an opening in the body, they have generally supposed that contact with food was what caused the secretion of the digestive fluids.

As a matter of fact, it has since been demonstrated that "if the operator had washed his hands, so that there were no odors of food on them capable of exciting the desire of the animal," no digestive fluids would have appeared.

Pavlov, to whose experiments we referred in another place, has shown that the secretions of the stomach vary according to the taste of the food, and that the digestive fluids are prepared while the food is still in the mouth. The sub consciousness of the mind, without your knowing it, warns the digestive organs in advance and they prepare beforehand the appropriate chemical re-agents.

Consequently, it is a scientific fact capable of physical proof that it is the mental picture, the appetite, the delectable taste, the mental desire, the enjoyment and appreciation of the food, that stimulates the digestive apparatus to perform its functions.

We have drawn our illustration from the digestive organs because the action of the mind upon them is most apparent. But the principle holds true with every form of functional derangement. There is apparently no disease, not even a germ disease, that cannot be caused, or at least simulated, through mental influence.

FUNDAMENTAL PRINCIPLES OF FUNCTIONAL HEALTH

This is made peculiarly evident during the prevalence of epidemics, when the cases caused by fear, imagination and belief manifest all the symptoms of true disease, excepting that they lack the distinguishing germ or bacillus.

Now, it is obvious that if the mind has power to cause a given organ to act in an abnormal or perverted manner, it must also have the power to restore that organ to normal operation.

In other words, —

Any disease that can be caused by the mind can be avoided by the mind.

You must recognize and believe the truth of four fundamental statements, and in order to emphasize them we repeat them categorically:

1. The immediate cause of abnormal or perverted action by any bodily, organ is abnormal or perverted mental action.

2. A plentiful supply of blood is necessary to the continued life and health of the body.

3. To stimulate any particular organ to special activity we must bring about an increased circulation of blood in the part indicated.

4. Any disease that can be caused by the mind can be avoided by the mind.

With these basic principles before us, we may consider the two fields of their application.

There are two kinds of people in the world — those who think they are perfectly well and those who think they are ailing. The former want to retain, and the latter to regain, health.

We shall therefore approach the subject of mental control of bodily functions, first, from the point of view of the preservation of health — that is to say, the prevention of disease — and, secondly, from the point of view of the cure of disease.

AVOIDANCE OF DISEASE

Chapter V

AVOIDANCE OF DISEASE

SOURCES OF FUNCTIONAL DISORDER

THERE would seem to be two ways in which functional disease may be avoided: first, by avoiding the states of mind that tend to produce it; second, by cultivating contrary states of mind.

Now, the states of mind that produce disease are those in which the aspects of disease are dwelt upon.

All consciousness is creative. No image can be held in consciousness without a coexistent associated motor impulse prompting the bodily action that would tend to make the image a reality.

Not that the mere thought of a disease will cause its immediate appearance.

But that the constant thinking of symptoms will release the energies that tend to their development.

Therefore, if you would be assured of health, avoid the subject of disease. Avoid reading, talking or thinking about abnormal conditions of the human body. Never allow such ideas to enter your mind. If they are thrust upon you by another, banish them with his presence.

Above all, avoid the sort of bodily introspection that looks for symptoms of disease similar to those of others. Those who practice this sort of thing are sure to find what they are looking for. And the more definite in the mind the object of search, the more certain the finding.

Ignore the remarks of others about the harmful effects of certain foods upon them. If there is nothing hurtful nor indigestible in the inherent character of the food itself, your own judgment must tell you that it is digestible and fit for food, and that the fault lies with the mental bias of the dyspeptic.

Every thought of bodily derangement is a - prolific source of functional disorder.

Hence, the beliefs created in your mind by the mistakes and falsehoods of others may be productive of dire consequences.

STEPS IN HEALTH'S STAIRWAY

Be ever on the watch. Post your attention as a sentinel to guard the gates of consciousness. We have said that there seem to be two ways in which the effect of adverse mental influences upon the body may be avoided. Yet in reality there is but one.

For so long as consciousness is under the control of the waking will it is never empty.

It demands incessant food for thought.

And the best way to avoid pernicious thoughts is to keep your consciousness busy with beneficent ones.

There are two steps in the stairway to perfect automatic functional health.

The first step is to supply the material necessaries of life. Know that your body requires at least two quarts of water in some form every day, that it requires fresh air, deep breathing, cleanliness, exercise and sleep, and that it requires food of the quantity and quality that the average man eats and enjoys.

The second step is to think stimulating thoughts. By stimulating thoughts we mean such thoughts as will prompt the organs of the body to transform the necessaries of life into flesh and bone and to discard the waste.

Stimulating thoughts are thoughts of health and well-being.

Whatever you do, do it with the serene conviction that it is good for you.

ENJOYMENT AND ASSIMILATION

Whatever you eat, be assured that it is nourishing and digestible. If you have this idea firmly implanted in your mind, if vou really believe it, you will enjoy your food whatever it may be. And tasting and enjoyment, the appreciation of delectable flavors, will be accompanied by thorough mastication and by the secretion of all the necessary digestive fluids.

No man can thrive upon an article of diet that he does not relish. Any well man will thrive upon any article of diet as long as he thoroughly enjoys it.

If you have perfect health, we have given you all that you need to know to avoid functional disease. And the less anxious thought you give to the state of your body the less likely will you be to contract disease. For every thought tends to work its own fulfilment.

BODILY SERENITY AND EFFICIENCY

Health implies bodily serenity. You cannot be healthy if you are seeking health.

Health is a state of physiological efficiency. It is a condition that is to be realized.

If you have health, you are in health, and health is in you. To keep mind and body in this state of harmony and working efficiency, all that you need do is to exercise a little common sense and obey these simple rules:

NINE RULES FOR KEEPING WELL

1. Think only those thoughts about your body that you desire to see realized in your body.

2. Think and talk health, and fix your mind in grateful serenity upon the assurance of your own immunity from disease. By so doing you will not only safeguard yourself, but you will suggest healthful and creative thoughts to others.

3. Steel yourself against all thoughts adverse to health that may be suggested to you by what you see or hear.

4. If such ideas are forced upon your attention, combat them with thoughts of your own strength, vitality and assured immunity from sickness.

5. In the presence of the sick, do not waste your time and their strength discussing pains and symptoms. Such thoughts will only emphasize the symptoms and aggravate the illness. Instead, talk and think Hope, Convalescence and Health. Get creative ideas into the sick man's mind instead of destructive ideas. And when you are out of his presence rejoice, for your own self-preservation, in your own bodily health and freedom from pain.

6. Do not allow your friends to tell you their troubles. Make them tell you of their improvement and their expectations of health.

7. Eat all the food you can enjoy. The kind is immaterial so long as you are really convinced that it tastes good and that you can assimilate it.

8. Get plenty of fresh air, exercise and sleep; practice deep breathing and cleanliness and be regular in your habits.

9. Drink at least two quarts of water, in some form every day.

If you adhere strictly to these rules, the functional health you now enjoy is yours for the rest of your natural life.

And if any functional disorder should ever come upon you, you can ascribe it directly to your own disobedience of some one or more of those injunctions.

PSYCHOTHERAPEUTICS

Chapter VI

PSYCHOTHERAPEUTICS

VAGARIES OF HEALTH CULTS

HERE remains the other class of men and women in the world — those who are ailing. And this brings us to the employment of mental powers in the cure of disease.

It will be well to restate the basic principles agreed upon at the outset of our discussion of bodily health as at factor in personal efficiency.

1. The immediate cause of abnormal perverted action by any bodily organ is abnormal or perverted mental action.

2. A plentiful supply of blood is necessary to the continued life and health of the body.

3. To stimulate any particular organ to special activity we must bring about an increased circulation of blood in the part indicated.

4. Any disease that can be caused by the mind can be avoided by the mind.

While mind and body are mutually inter-dependent, they are not identical.

This seems so obvious as to require no statement. Yet there are those who become so absorbed in Christian Science, Suggestion, New Thought and isms as to believe that health is solely a matter of mind, of thought, of faith.

The number who allow their judgment to be thus swayed by credulity is vast. Whole sects maintain that opinion. Consequently, it is not surprising that in so many cases they meet with failure that is to them inexplicable.

The reason lies in the insufficiency of a philosophy that ignores the fact that the body is part of the world of matter and dependent for its life upon the continued supply of material constituents.

An abundance of good food, good water and good air is just as necessary to regain health as to retain it. If no well man could thrive on the mincing diet of the habitual dyspeptic, certainly no sick man could get well on it.

First, then, every sufferer must conform to the requirements we have laid down for the healthy man.

So, if you are in anything but perfect health, turn back and study them again.

DIRECTIONS FOR STIMULATING ORGANIC ACTIVITY

Do not wait for more information.

Do not wait for more details about how to drink and eat and breathe.

The way to resume normal habits of life is to resume.

If the water that you drink is fit to drink at all, it is fit to drink in ample quantities.

If you do not enjoy the food you eat, get something else that is ordinarily considered good and wholesome and that you can enjoy.

If you are not getting enough fresh air, do not wait to learn the best system of breathing exercises. Just breathe in all the fresh air that your lungs will hold as often as you can in the way that most refreshes you, and let it go at that.

So, also, as to your mental attitude.

It is absolutely essential that you should carry out in your mental life the rules we have laid down.

But if you are a sufferer, if any organ is failing in its duty, you must do more. You must also stimulate that organ to increased activity.

There is but one way of accomplishing this, and that is by devoting part of your time to deliberate and systematic concentration of your mental energies.

We have already prescribed the method for doing this in Volume Ten. We repeat the directions here with appropriate variations.

First — Every night, half an hour before retiring, go to your room, where you can be entirely alone and as remote as possible from every sort of noise and distraction.

Second — Seat yourself in a wide and comfortable chair, or, better still, lie down on your back at full length. See that your clothing is loosened, so that you will suffer no distracting annoyance on this account. Compose yourself as if for sleep, assuming a position of restfulness, abandon, and utter relaxation. Close your eyes, letting the lids rest lightly on your check.

Third — Shut your mind resolutely against every form of bodily sensation. Forget for the time that you are encumbered with a body.

Fourth — Bar out of your consciousness every memory, every thought of the past .

Fifth — Place your hand over the organ of your body that you desire to influence.

Form a mental picture of that organ. Observe its operation. Visualize it, feel it, see it, as part of yourself, as being a part of your body at that moment.

Call upon it to do its work vigorously.

Compel mentally a concentration of blood in the organ that requires stimulation.

Close your mind against everything except the thought that the blood is leaving other portions of your body and is swelling the arteries and capillaries of the special organ.

As you do this you will gradually feel through your fingers a comfortable sensation of heat and warmth in that part of your body.

You may then know that your consciousness has come into rapport with the sluggish organ, and that you will have no further trouble from that source.

It has been simply a question of pointing out to an individually intelligent part of your organism just where it was failing in its duty and of restoring a harmonious and co-operative efficiency in your body.

Dwell with joyful satisfaction upon the thought that your troubles are over that at last you are to have perfect health.

Think what a relief it is to realize that you need never again wonder if that organ which has been troubling you in the past is going to perform its duty.

Now you know that it will never again be the source of pain or anxiety.

Exult in your deliverance. Rejoice that you are now free to let yourself go, to relax your vigilance, to release all strains and tensions.

Devote not less than thirty minutes to this fifth exercise.

Sixth — Arise and make your preparations for the night. Then, upon retiring, again close your eyes and repeat for five or ten minutes the procedure set out under the fifth instruction.

Seventh — Every time you are awake during the night call before your mind's eye the mental picture of the bodily organ that needs stimulating and see it in vigorous operation. Hold this thought steadfastly in consciousness as long as you remain awake.

Eighth — In the morning, with the first dawning of consciousness, repeat the procedure set out in the third, fourth and fifth instructions.

These instructions are necessarily vague. We even hesitate to give them, because we realize that they are so lacking in specific directions with reference to particular organs and functions as to be of value chiefly for their suggestional effect. They are not intended to do more than illustrate the principle.

Nor will any procedure accomplish its purpose if followed in a merely perfunctory manner.

THE EFFICIENT THERAPEUTIC CONSCIOUSNESS

The mental picture that you hold must be more than a flat and toneless mechanical drawing.

It must be vitalized in Faith. Its elements must stand out in life-like perspective. They must possess a throbbing reality.

For the efficient consciousness, as we have frequently pointed out, is not composed of mere ideas. It is composed of beliefs in ideas and ideas that are believed in. And your mental picture must be conceived in unwavering Faith.

ILLUSTRATIVE CASES OF PARTICULAR AILMENTS

The ailments in which mental concentration is most conspicuously successful are those marked by pain, sleeplessness, nausea, derangements of the digestive and eliminating processes, extreme nervous irritability, melancholy, spasms, evil habits and moral obliquities. Among these are the following specific diseases which we cite as peculiarly susceptible to treatment by mental control:

Insomnia, hysteria, habit pains and tremors, hysterical muscle contractions, profuse sweating, appetites for unnatural foods (such as clay gluttony) y lack of appetite, liquor and drug habits, delusions, obsessions, morbid fears, sexual perversions and weaknesses, kleptomania, seasickness, constipation, indigestion, dyspepsia, headache, biliousness and goitre.

The following illustrations are actually reported cases of cures effected wholly by mental treatment.

These cases are reported by men eminent in the medical profession, most of whom occupy chairs in leading universities.

We can give but a few of these cases, and those briefly, in order to keep this volume within reasonable limits.

Neuralgia. — The sufferer in this case was a man forty-five years of age, who had been operated on twice for trifacial neuralgia. Each operation had been followed by a year of comparative freedom from pain, after which the pain returned. The only remedy that medicine or surgery could offer was the removal of the ganglion. His condition when he began mental treatment was such that when he tried to speak the muscles of one side of his face would contract in a violent spasm attended by, extreme pain. He could eat only liquid food because of the pain involved in the movement of his jaws in chewing, and he was condemned to almost constant silence by the pain of speech. From the first day of his employment of mental methods of treatment he was relieved. He had no pain after the fourth day. And on the tenth day he found himself entirely cured.

Insomnia. — A business disaster, long continued overwork, and incessant anxiety had so preyed on a man thirty-seven years old that for months he had been unable to sleep more than three or four hours out of the twenty-four. He read most of the night to keep his mind off his troubles. He had no appetite. He felt and looked like a sick man. He was pale, haggard and worn. His was a difficult case; because the business cares that had been the exciting cause of his insomnia were still weighing upon him. On the very first night that he began mental treatment he slept from ten o'clock at night until seven in the morning. The following night was a restless one. But after ten days of the practice of concentrative methods he had no further trouble.

Constipation. — Mr. was a self-centered, sour-visaged and irritable old man who suffered continually from pain in the rectum. For more than twenty years he had taken an enema every day. He had been afraid to go without one for a single day. He consented to try mental concentration. He was cured from the first day, and though many years have elapsed he has never again been troubled with constipation.

Gastro- Intestinal Dyspepsia. — A lawyer, thirty-six years old, had so suffered from this disease that he had lost seventy-five pounds in weight, was a mere framework of a man and weak as an infant. His breath was foul and his tongue coated. Even a very small quantity of milk caused severe gastric troubles. His case had resisted all the medications of an expert and prudent physician, who had employed every possible weapon of materia medica to combat the disease. In five weeks under mental treatment he gained thirtyfive pounds.

Tachycardia (Palpitation of the Heart). — A young woman, twenty-six years of age, a trifle thin, but apparently in good general health, was subject to nightly seizures of palpitation of the heart accompanied by trembling and a terrifying feeling that she was about to die. Her husband was greatly alarmed about her and called two physicians into consultation. Despite their efforts the attacks became more frequent and the patient was in momentary expectation of death. After one month of mental treatment her cure was complete.

Functional Paralysis. — An emotional woman became subject to palpitation of the heart. She lost all appetite for food, was troubled with insomnia, and gradually lost the use of her lower limbs. When she commenced mental measures of treatment she was a confirmed invalid. She was cured in a few days.

THE KERNEL OF THERAPEUTIC TRUTH

It is unnecessary to cite further illustrations of this kind.

Faith in your own self-mastery is the kernel of truth. Faith is the vitalizing element in all mental measures for the cure of disease.

And Faith, to be efficient, must he directed toward a specific ideal.

And Faith is Concentration — concentration of consciousness upon a possessing thought.

Such concentration must necessarily evolve its emotional element, Desire.

And Desire evolved through Concentration, backed by Faith, and intelligently directed, can never fail to preserve or to restore Functional Health.